SAN DIEGO WOMEN'S HAGGADAH
Second Edition

SAN DIEGO WOMEN'S HAGGADAH
Second Edition

Woman's Institute For Continuing Jewish Education

Woman's Institute for Continuing Jewish Education
4126 Executive Drive, La Jolla, CA 92037

First Edition   *First Printing 1980*
                 Second Printing 1984
Second Edition   *First Printing 1986*
                 Second Printing 1990
                 Third Printing 1993

Copyright © 1986 Woman's Institute For Continuing
Jewish Education. All rights reserved. No part of this
book may be used or reproduced in any manner without
written permission except in the case of brief quotations
contained in critical articles and reviews.

Library of Congress Card Number: 85-51376
ISBN 09608054-5-1

This Haggadah is a product of the cooperative work of:

Betsy Arnold
Miriam Bauer
Irene Fine
Randee Friedman
Helen Gotkowitz
Sylvia Karzen
Debby Kremsdorf
Barbara Rosen
Arlene Saidman
Jeannie Steiger
Jacquelyn Tolley
Jane Sprague Zones, editor

THE SAN DIEGO WOMEN'S HAGGADAH
Second Edition

Preface to the Second Edition

One year after forming the Woman's Institute for Continuing Jewish Education, we decided to set aside one evening during Passover to hold a women's Seder. This would be a time when women could sit down, share a meal and recite stories about their liberation in terms of the exodus from Egypt. The seventh night was designated for this occasion because it was removed from the celebration of family Seders during the first and second nights of Passover. This would indeed be a time when we could rest and recline as free women.

Scheduling the event was easy. Finding an Haggadah to read in connection with the Seder was difficult. We needed a text that would include women's stories. We searched in vain; there was none in print. Finally, in the absence of an adequate Haggadah, we decided to write our own. We could surround this important event, the liberation from bondage, with our own stories concerning freedom. We could tell, and retell, the roles of our foremothers as well as those of our forefathers. We could bring to the reader's eyes and ears glorious tales never

vii

before told at a Passover meal. The result of that research and writing became the first *San Diego Women's Haggadah.*

From our modest beginnings in 1979, the women's Seder has become an important event in San Diego. We have grown in number from 27 women meeting in private homes to 75 celebrating together in the social hall of a local synagogue. Our meals have changed from the original potluck variety to a light catered repast — for many of us a true sign of liberation.

Traditions connected with our Seder have evolved. For instance, an unusual way of keeping a permanent record of this special event was designed. The name of the leader of each Seder is elegantly embroidered on a large pillow, which then becomes the cushion against which the leader reclines.

The Seder has become an intergenerational affair. Mothers, daughters and grandmothers sit down together and share stories of previous Passovers, many of which were held in different countries where foods and traditions varied. As our after-dinner entertainment, we read the winning entries from our annual writing contest. We also award the customary prize for finding the afikomen: one tuition-free class the following year at the Institute.

Over the years the Seder has become an unusual learning experience for many of us. Anybody from the community can volunteer to lead the Seder. If she has never done so before, then the leader from the previous year coaches her in the procedure. In this way, any woman who desires can have the opportunity to conduct a community Seder. We have been told that for many, this activity of leadership is truly a liberating experience. Instructive "Notes to the Leader of the Seder" are printed at the end of this book.

As a result of all this creativity and productivity surrounding our annual event, we decided to update the original Haggadah and include some of the new materials collected since the first edition. We know that this new work, which is a record of our growth and development, will also mirror the growth of those who read the second edition. To this end, we have asked that readers please join in and add their share, whether it be in story, song or prayer. Let's all make this women's Haggadah a dynamic on-going process in celebrating Jewish freedom.

Irene Fine
San Diego, California

Acknowledgements

We would like to thank the following people whose generous contributions helped make the publication of this book possible:

In memory of Muriel Fisch
  Betsy Arnold
Honoring my parents, Ann and Robert Rivers
  Eileen Bachrach
In honor of all the creative women of the Institute
  Miriam Bauer
Rabbi Lenore Bohm
Barbara Brandt
In gratitude for my loving memories of my mothers,
Rose Segal and Sara Cushman, and my grandmother,
Etta Levenson
  Fran Cushman
In loving tribute to my mother, Sylvia Bedell Sandler
  Bonnie Feinman
In honor of our mothers, Sadie Fink and Rose Fine
  Irene and Larry Fine
Honoring Andrew Samuel Friedman and Barry Joel
Friedman
  Randee Friedman
Hanna Gleiberman
In honor of Stephany Andelson Goldzband
  Marilyn Goldzband
Dr. Paul Goodman
In honor of my mother, Fannie Alperin
  Helen Gotkowitz
In honor of my loving children, Eric, Jennifer and Brian
  Joani Gross
Barbara Hurwitz
Debby Kalish

In honor of Robin Amy Kremsdorf
    Richard and Debby Kremsdorf
Ruth Lipton
In memory of my parents, Sarah and Hyman Yaffe
    Freda Yaffe Magid
In honor of Jeffrey Lee Polinsky
    Viviana Polinsky
To honor our daughter and granddaughters, Genine,
Marisa and Amber Hallsted
    Dona Shenkman
In honor of our children, Jonathan and Jeffrey
    Brooke and Lewis Stern
Jacquelyn Tolley

THE SAN DIEGO WOMEN'S HAGGADAH
Second Edition

Kadeish
(sanctifying the day)

קַדֵּשׁ

Tonight we celebrate the story of the Jewish people, who are linked throughout time with all peoples in the passion for justice and human liberty. As is traditional in this annual feast of liberation, we give thanks for the preservation of our spirit in the face of challenge and threat. We give thanks for the event that became our great symbol of liberation — the Exodus from Egypt. We give thanks for the inspiration that taught us to live by law. And we give thanks for the first laws which proclaim the dignity of human beings: the Ten Commandments, Torah, and Shabbat.

This is a special evening, one that our ancestors would not have anticipated in a thousand years! We gather tonight as Jewish women to celebrate as well the special part that women have played in Jewish liberation.

We begin by reciting the moving poem, "Blessed Is the Match," by Hannah Senesh.

Blessed Is the Match

Blessed is the match
   consumed in kindling flame.
Blessed is the flame
   that burns in the secret
   fastness of the heart.
Blessed is the heart
   with strength to stop
   its beating for honor's sake.
Blessed is the match
   consumed in kindling flame.

THE CANDLES ARE LIT AND THE
FOLLOWING BLESSING IS RECITED.

בָּרוּךְ אַתָּה יְיָ אֱלֹהֵינוּ מֶלֶךְ הָעוֹלָם אֲשֶׁר קִדְּשָׁנוּ בְּמִצְוֹתָיו וְצִוָּנוּ
לְהַדְלִיק נֵר שֶׁל (שַׁבָּת וְשֶׁל) יוֹם טוֹב.

Baruch Ata, Adonai Eloheinu,
melech ha-olam, asher kid'shanu
b'mitsvotav v'tsivanu l'hadlik
neir shel (shabat veshel) yom tov.

Blessed are You, our God, Creator
of the Universe, who makes us holy
with mitzvot and commands us to
kindle the (Sabbath and) festival
lights.

Hannah Senesh is a daughter of the exodus, as are all of us here tonight. Torah teaches us that the God of Israel despised slavery, and that we are God's agents to free all human beings from the bonds that limit them. We learn from the Book of Exodus that deliverance comes with our refusal to accept injustice. In Exodus the first steps toward freedom for the Hebrew people were taken by women. Midwives defied Pharaoh to preserve new lives. Pharaoh's daughter plotted with slave women to adopt a Hebrew child, whom she called Moses. The first to scorn oppression, women took the initiative which led to liberation.

Kiddush

EVERYONE RAISES HER FIRST CUP OF WINE, AS THE FOLLOWING BLESSING IS RECITED.

בָּרוּךְ אַתָּה יְיָ אֱלֹהֵינוּ מֶלֶךְ הָעוֹלָם בּוֹרֵא פְּרִי הַגָּפֶן: ④

בָּרוּךְ אַתָּה, יְיָ אֱלֹהֵינוּ, מֶלֶךְ הָעוֹלָם, אֲשֶׁר בָּחַר בָּנוּ מִכָּל together
עָם, וְרוֹמְמָנוּ מִכָּל לָשׁוֹן, וְקִדְּשָׁנוּ בְּמִצְוֹתָיו. וַתִּתֶּן־לָנוּ, יְיָ
אֱלֹהֵינוּ, בְּאַהֲבָה (שַׁבָּתוֹת לִמְנוּחָה וּ)מוֹעֲדִים לְשִׂמְחָה, חַגִּים
וּזְמַנִּים לְשָׂשׂוֹן, אֶת יוֹם (הַשַּׁבָּת הַזֶּה, וְאֶת יוֹם) חַג הַמַּצוֹת הַזֶּה,
זְמַן חֵרוּתֵנוּ, (בְּאַהֲבָה) מִקְרָא קֹדֶשׁ, זֵכֶר לִיצִיאַת מִצְרָיִם. כִּי
בָנוּ בָחַרְתָּ, וְאוֹתָנוּ קִדַּשְׁתָּ מִכָּל הָעַמִּים, (וְשַׁבָּת) וּמוֹעֲדֵי
קָדְשְׁךָ (בְּאַהֲבָה וּבְרָצוֹן) בְּשִׂמְחָה וּבְשָׂשׂוֹן הִנְחַלְתָּנוּ. בָּרוּךְ
אַתָּה, יְיָ, מְקַדֵּשׁ (הַשַּׁבָּת וְ)יִשְׂרָאֵל וְהַזְּמַנִּים.

Baruch Ata, Adonai Eloheinu, melech ha-olam,
borei p'ri hagafen. Baruch Ata, Adonai Eloheinu,
melech haolam, asher bachar banu mikol am,
v'rom'manu mikol lashon, v'kid'shanu b'mitsvotav.
Vatiten lanu Adonai Eloheinu b'ahava (shabatot
lim'nucha u) moadim l'sim'cha chagim uz'manim
l'sason et yom (hashabat hazeh v'et yom) chag hamatsot
hazeh z'man cheiruteinu (b'ahava) mik'ra kodesh
zeicher litsiat Mits'rayim. Ki vanu vachar'ta v'otanu
kidash'ta mikol ha-amim (v'shabat) umoadei kod'sh'cha
(b'ahava uv'ratson) b'sim'cha uv'sason hin'chal'tanu.
Baruch Ata, Adonai, m'kadeish (hashabat v') Yisraeil
v'haz'manim.

Blessed are You, our God, Sovereign of the Universe,
Creator of the fruit of the vine.

Blessed are You, our God, Creator of the Universe, who selected us from among all people and gave us Your commandments. Lovingly you have given us (Sabbaths for rest,) times for joy, seasons for celebration, and this feast of Matsa for the anniversary of our becoming free — a remembrance of our release from Egypt. Blessed are You, our God, who sanctifies (the Sabbath,) Israel and the holidays.

Now we say the blessing that reminds us of the continuous wonder of being alive — the shehecheyanu, a prayer usually said only on "first nights". Because this is our first coming together as women at this season, it is appropriate for us to acknowledge our reunion after long absence.

ALL:

בָּרוּךְ אַתָּה יְיָ, אֱלֹהֵינוּ מֶלֶךְ הָעוֹלָם, שֶׁהֶחֱיָנוּ,
וְקִיְּמָנוּ, וְהִגִּיעָנוּ לַזְּמַן הַזֶּה.

Baruch Ata, Adonai Eloheinu, melech ha-olam,
shehecheyanu, v'kiy'manu, v'higi-anu laz'man hazeh.

Blessed are You, our God, Creator of the Universe,
who has given us life and sustenance, has kept us alive,
and has brought us to this moment.

EVERYONE DRINKS THE
FIRST CUP OF WINE.

Ur'chats
(washing hands)

CEREMONIAL WASHING OF HANDS
BY LEADER.

Even before the Exodus from Egypt, each spring our people celebrated creation and the mystery of life. As we did then, we now remind ourselves that both the tender greens of the earth and the salts of the sea are joined together to sustain life. We remind ourselves that in slavery the salt of our tears released our strength to survive.

Like all people, our people in ancient times celebrated the liberation of the earth itself from wintery darkness and rejoiced in the yearly rebirth of nature. This is beautifully described in the Song of Songs (2:10-13):

My beloved spoke,
and said unto me:
"Rise up, my love,
my fair one, and come away,
For lo, the winter is past,
The rain is over and gone;
The flowers appear on the earth;
The time of singing is come,
And the voice of the turtle is
heard in our land;
The fig tree puts forth her green figs,
And the vines in blossom give
forth their fragrance.
Arise, my love, my fair one,
and come away."

KUMI LACH

Words--Song
of Songs 2:10-11

Music by
Debbie Friedman

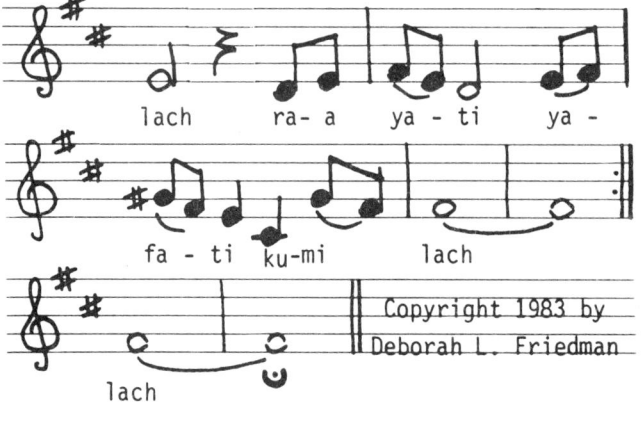

lach ra- a ya - ti ya -
fa - ti ku-mi lach
lach

Copyright 1983 by
Deborah L. Friedman

Karpas
(eating greens dipped in salt water)

בַּרְפַּס

EVERYONE TAKES A PORTION OF GREENS,
AND EACH PERSON DIPS HER GREENS IN
SALT WATER. ALL RECITE THE BLESSING:

בָּרוּךְ אַתָּה יְיָ, אֱלֹהֵינוּ מֶלֶךְ הָעוֹלָם, בּוֹרֵא פְּרִי
הָאֲדָמָה.

Baruch Ata, Adonai Eloheinu, melech ha-olam
borei p'ri ha-adama.

Blessed are You, our God, Sovereign of the Universe,
Creator of the fruit of the earth.

EAT GREENS DIPPED IN SALT WATER

Yachats
(breaking the middle matsa)

יַחַץ

ONE PERSON UNCOVERS THE MATSOT

The four matsot before me represent the pascal lamb,
the people of Israel, the power of women, and hope for
the freedom of all Jewish people, particularly those still
living in tyranny and oppression.

Since the Passover sacrifice of a lamb was no longer
possible after the destruction of the second Temple in
70 C.E., a matsa, in addition to the bone, came to represent the lamb.

SOMEONE BREAKS A MIDDLE MATSA AND
PLACES ONE PART BACK UNDER THE COVER.

First it is the custom to divide the matsa of freedom in two. One part we keep here with the rest of the matsot. The second part, called the afikoman, we hide. After the meal, we will hunt for it and the finder will be rewarded. When the hidden part is found, we will put the two halves together again, and this will be a sign that what is broken off is not really lost to our people, as long as WE remember and search. Each of us will then eat a bit of the ceremonial matsa, in place of the lamb eaten in the days of the Temple.

Maggid
(telling the story)

מַגִּיד

SOMEONE HOLDS ALOFT THE PLATE WITH
THE UNCOVERED MATSOT.

Now we repeat the call to Passover.

Lets say together

ALL:
   This is the bread of affliction which our
ancestors ate in the land of Egypt. Let all who
are hungry come and eat! Whoever is in need,
come and celebrate the Passover. Now here,
next year in the land of Israel. Now enslaved,
next year daughters of freedom!

SET DOWN THE MATSA PLATE.
FILL THE SECOND CUP OF WINE.

The Four Questions

 Tonight we have gathered our foremothers to the table, to surround our story with their commentary. Just as the Talmud brings together the thinking of rabbis from all ages as if they were present at a single discussion — so we bring together our foremothers.

For Our Mothers

We speak of Deborah,
our mother, of Beruriah
and Hannah and Gluckel;

Of all our mothers whose strength
And courage and faith in our God
above and around and within
Enabled us to reach this day.

We question our foremothers;
and they reply.

Mother, we ask, *why is this night different from all other nights? Why do we celebrate a women's Seder?*

Deborah, judge and prophetess, "who arose a mother of Israel" [Judges 5:7], considers this question carefully.

The only woman judge in the ancient nation of Israelites, Deborah held court under a palm tree outside her home lest anyone accuse her of impropriety. For it was said that a woman must not be alone in her home with a man other than her husband.

Deborah had also promoted the war of liberation against King Jabin of Canaan, who continued to oppress the Israelite settlements with his superior weaponry of iron chariots. Appointing Barak as military commander, she shrewdly directed the campaign, taking advantage of flood conditions to mire the opponents' iron chariots. The entire enemy camp was destroyed, and the victory, recorded in the Song of Deborah, ushered in a 40-year period of peace for Israel. Nevertheless, rabbis, recording in the Aggadah, saw Deborah as arrogant and boastful and gave her the unflattering name of "Devorah", meaning "bee".

This is the reply Deborah gives to our first question:
"They called me a judge in Israel. They called me a woman of great and rare distinction, a mother of my nation. And yet when they came to me for advice, to draw on that wisdom and compassion of which they were in such awe, they made me leave my home and sit outside. For in their eyes all women were the same, weak and wanton, not to be trusted alone in the company of men.

"We celebrate a women's Seder tonight so that we are free to be ourselves, not afraid that our actions will be misjudged or misinterpreted, considered bold or unwomanly."

We turn now to Beruriah. *Mother, we ask, why do we taste this bitterness and keep it fresh in our mouths?*

Beruriah was the daughter of Rabbi Ben Teradyon and wife of Rabbi Meir, both respected scholars who supported her study of Torah and Sanhedrin law. So highly regarded was Beruriah's scholarship that her opinions became part of halacha, an extraordinary occurrence in those times and not common even today.

It is told of Beruriah that she rebuked her husband when he prayed for the death of certain evil persons. "God seeks the eradication of sin, not sinners," she said, and exhorted her husband to pray for the sinners to give up their evil ways. Her incisive mind sometimes led her to reply sharply and she was known for her quick retorts.

"My life," explains Beruriah in answer to our question, "has been both sweet and bitter. The sweetness needs little explanation. It flows from Torah, the study of which is a blessing. The bitterness is equally evident. The scholars considered my degree of learning to be astonishing for a woman. Brilliant as they were, these learned men never realized that any woman, given the same opportunity, might have become my equal...or theirs.

"Be reminded at this celebration of freedom, that freedom must be won again by every generation. You, too, must make your exodus from Egypt."

10 And now we ask, *Mother, why then do we taste both salt tears and sweet?*

Hannah Senesh knows the answer to our question. She knows it well.

Born in Hungary in 1921 and shot in 1941 at the age of twenty, Hannah Senesh had been an exceptional child, admitted to a special private school where Jews were rarely allowed. When voted president of the school's literary society, she was disqualified for the position because of her religion. The episode crystalized her feeling that Jews could be free only in the land of Israel.

Hannah became an ardent Zionist, and when she arrived in Palestine at age seventeen, she fell in love with the land and its people. She felt a sense of destiny, that she had a mission to fulfill. This inner calling to service led to her enlistment with a special military unit that was to warn Jews in Hungary of Hitler's lethal plans. Members of the unit were parachuted into Yugoslavia and from there, made their way by foot into Hungary. Hannah Senesh was caught, tortured and put to death — but not before she was able to give hope to many other suffering prisoners.

This is Hannah's answer to our third question:

"I shed many tears in my short life; tears of frustration over the opportunities denied to me because of my religion, tears of fear during my secret mission, tears of pain at the hands of my tormentors and, at the end, tears of grief, for I loved my life and did not want it to end.

"Yet through all the salty tears, the sweet beauty of the land and the people of Palestine sustained me. As long as it exists I will be there, basking in its sweetness."

We address the fourth question to Glückel of Hameln. *Mother, why do we find it so difficult to lean back and relax during this meal?*

Glückel had lived a long and full life. She was born in Hamburg, daughter of a prominent family, and at fourteen, she married. Later, as wife and mother of twelve children, she also advised her husband on business matters so that when he died, leaving her with eight of their twelve children still under her care, she was able to continue the family's financial enterprises. Later Glückel married again.

Her melancholy over her first husband's death led Glückel to write her memoirs. She never saw herself as an unusual woman, but attributed her good fortune to God and said she merely followed the path God chose for her.

"Now," Glückel tells us, "is the season to relish our freedom, to reign as queens in our own homes. I bore twelve children,nurtured them to adulthood, and provided for their material needs after the death of my husband. Rest was a rare and precious commodity for me.

"Yet I found even my few moments of leisure difficult to enjoy. Women are the ones who create and sustain, and so we can never truly be at rest. There will always be needs, always be cares; and you and I will always have to be there, daughter, to help, to heal, and to nurture."

There are stars whose radiance is
visible on earth
though they have
long been extinct.
There are people whose brilliance
continues to light the world
though they are no
longer among the living.
These lights are particularly
bright when the night is dark.
They light the way for
[hu]mankind.

Hannah Senesh

The Four Daughters

13
Four daughters: one wise, one bitter, one simple and one who does not know how to question, come to sit among their mothers.

Four daughters of Deborah, Beruriah, Glückel and Hannah sit and learn of their Passover inheritance.

"Mothers," asks the wise daughter, "What has the Shekhina* commanded us on this night?"

Her mothers respond: "We must tell of our fore-mothers' part in the exodus from Egypt, for their story has been excluded. And we, all of us, must resolve to tell our story tonight and on all Passover nights to come."

The bitter daughter asks: "Why are you, mere women, talking of things that demand intelligent discussion and thought?"

By saying "you" instead of "we", this daughter alienates herself from the company of women. By demeaning women's intelligence, she keeps herself in a position of inferiority.

Her mothers point this out to her: "By excluding yourself from our community of women, you ignore that which Miriam did for all of us, and continue to enslave

*"*Shekhina* is the frequently used Talmudic term denoting the visible and audible manifestation of God's presence on earth. In its ultimate development as it appears in the late Midrash literature, the Shekhina concept stood for an independent, feminine divine entity prompted by her compassionate nature to argue with God in defense of [man]."

Raphael Patai, *The Hebrew Goddess*, Avon Books, 1978, p. 99.

yourself with the old prejudices that were devised to weaken us."

The simple daughter asks, "What is it that Miriam did for us?"

The mothers reply, "Tonight we will tell you of Miriam's wisdom and her part in bringing us out of Egypt."

The fourth daughter,
who does not know how to
question, must be led
by the hand through the
exodus by her mothers
and sisters.

ALL:
Let us all be wise here, and full of questions. Everything in the Seder has meaning. Even if we were full of wisdom, venerable sages all, steeped in Torah, it would still be incumbent upon us to recount the exodus from Egypt and examine each word.

MA NISH'TANA

Israeli

Ma nish'ta-na ha - lai'la ha-zeh mi-

kol ha - lei - lot, mi- kol ha - lei -

lot? She-b' - chol haleilot a- nu och'lin cha-

meits u-ma - tsa, cha-meits u-ma-tsa. Ha-

lai'la ha - zeh, ha - lai'-la ha-zeh ku-

lo ma - tsa, ha-lai'la ha-zeh

ha - lai'la hazeh ku - lo ma-tsa. She-b'

22

מַה־נִּשְׁתַּנָּה הַלַּיְלָה הַזֶּה מִכָּל־הַלֵּילוֹת. שֶׁבְּכָל־הַלֵּילוֹת אָנוּ אוֹכְלִין
חָמֵץ וּמַצָּה. הַלַּיְלָה הַזֶּה כֻּלּוֹ מַצָּה.
שֶׁבְּכָל־הַלֵּילוֹת אָנוּ אוֹכְלִין שְׁאָר יְרָקוֹת. הַלַּיְלָה הַזֶּה מָרוֹר.
שֶׁבְּכָל־הַלֵּילוֹת אֵין אָנוּ מַטְבִּילִין אֲפִילוּ פַּעַם אֶחָת. הַלַּיְלָה הַזֶּה
שְׁתֵּי פְעָמִים.
שֶׁבְּכָל־הַלֵּילוֹת אָנוּ אוֹכְלִין בֵּין יוֹשְׁבִין וּבֵין מְסֻבִּין. הַלַּיְלָה הַזֶּה
כֻּלָּנוּ מְסֻבִּין.

2. Sheb'chol haleilot anu och'lin sh'ar y'rakot,
   halai'la hazeh maror.

3. Sheb'chol haleilot ein anu mat'bilin afilu pa-am
   echat, halai'la hazeh sh'tei f'amim.

4. Sheb'chol haleilot anu och'lin bein yosh'vin uvein
   m'subin, halai'la hazeh kulanu m'subin.

Why is this night different from
   all other nights?
On all other nights, we eat either
   leavened bread or matsa;
   on this night — only matsa.
On all other nights, we eat all
   kinds of herbs; on this night
   we especially eat bitter herbs.
On all other nights, we do not dip
   herbs at all; on this night
   we dip them twice.
On all other nights, we eat in an
   ordinary manner; tonight
   we dine with special ceremony.

Why on this night do we eat only matsot?

Avadot hayinu — we were slaves. We were slaves in the land of Egypt. Our mothers in their flight from bondage in Egypt did not have time to let the dough rise, so they baked flat bread, called matsa. The Bible tells us, "They were thrust out of Egypt and could not tarry, neither had they prepared for themselves any victuals" [Exodus 12:39]. In memory of this, we eat only matsot, no bread, during Passover.

Why on this night do we eat bitter herbs?

Avadot hayinu — we were slaves. We eat bitter herbs because the Egyptians made bitter the lives of our ancestors. The Bible tells us, "They made their lives bitter with hard service, in mortar and in brick, and in all manner of service in the field; in all their service wherein they made them serve with rigor" [Exodus 1:14].

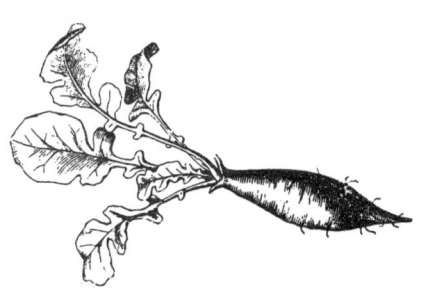

Why do we dip our greens twice?

Avadot hayinu — we were slaves. The first time we dip our greens to taste the brine of enslavement. But the second time, we dip to remind ourselves of all life and growth, of earth and sea, combined through divine power to give us sustenence.

The second time we shall dip in charoset, to remind ourselves of the mortar that our ancestors mixed as slaves to the Pharaohs in Egypt. But our charoset is a mixture of sweet fruits, nuts and wine, to show us that in their bitter time of slavery, our ancestors hoped for the sweet delights of freedom which we, as women, are tasting tonight.

Why do we recline while we eat?

Avadot hayinu — we were slaves. Reclining at the table was a sign of freedom in olden times. Since our ancestors were freed from slavery, we recline to remind ourselves that we, like our ancestors, can overcome bondage in our own time.

AVADOT HAYINU

Words by Randee Friedman
and Rabbi Lenore Bohm

Traditional music
for "Avadim Hayinu"

We were slaves.
Now we (women) are free.

We were pharaoh's slaves in Egypt. And the Lord brought us from there with a mighty hand and an outstretched arm. If the Holy One had not brought out our mothers and fathers from Egypt, then we, our daughters and sons, our children's children, would still have been slaves to Pharaoh in Egypt. Even if we were wise, all-sensible, experienced, and understanding of the Torah, it would still be our duty to tell of the departure from Egypt. The more one tells of the departure from Egypt, the more one is to be praised.

SOMEONE HOLDS UP THE EGG FROM THE PASSOVER PLATE.

After the escape from Egypt, the Israelites came into their promised land and built their Temple in Jerusalem. To the Temple they brought festival offerings, in thanksgiving for the fertility of their fields and flocks. This egg recalls such offerings. The egg is the symbol of life, and of growth and fruition.

SOMEONE HOLDS UP THE SHANK BONE.

This shank bone is the reminder of the Passover lamb, of the Divine instruction to the Hebrews in Egypt to sacrifice a lamb and mark their doorposts with its blood. This was a sign for the Angel of Death to pass over their houses and strike only Egyptians, to cause them to set free their slaves.

Again we ask ourselves, how did we become slaves in Egypt?

THE MOTHERS SPEAK IN TURN.

It is told that God spoke to Abraham and Sarah and told them to come to the other side of the Euphrates River so they could worship the one God. Sarah had a son, Isaac, and to Isaac and Rebekah were born twin sons, Jacob and Esau. To Esau and his descendents, God gave Mount Seir, and to Jacob and his descendents, God gave Canaan — the Promised Land.

Rachel, Jacob, Leah and Dina

And Jacob lived in the land and prospered and had many daughters and sons, but the sons of Jacob were jealous of their brother Joseph, for they felt he was favored by their father. They sold him into slavery in Egypt.

Then came a famine in the land, and Jacob and his family and their flocks went to Egypt in search of food, for they had heard that an official in Egypt had the foresight to store food in the event of famine. To their surprise, the official was their brother Joseph. And Joseph, seeing his kinfolk, helped them. This is how the children of Israel came to Egypt, where they lived and multiplied.

There arose a new king over Egypt who did not know Joseph. He told his people that the children of Israel were too many and too mighty. The king feared that in war the Israelites might turn against him.

"Therefore they did set over them taskmasters to afflict them with their burdens. And they built for Pharoah treasure cities, Pithom and Raamses...And they made their lives bitter with hard service, in mortar and in brick, and in all manner of service in the field... But the more they afflicted them, the more they multiplied and the more they spread abroad. And they were adread because of the children of Israel" [Exodus 1:11, 14, 12].

We were slaves. We dwelt in Egypt for 430 years.

It is customary at a Seder to recount the reasons we, as Jews, became slaves in Egypt. Tonight, we also ask how we, as women, became enslaved among our own people.

Some claim that from the beginning of human society there was a division of labor between women and men, arising out of biological differences between the sexes.

But this is not correct. In ancient times of simple, cooperative societies, we were the equals of men. Our reproductive abilities became the excuse, but are not the true reason for our being oppressed.

In the time after the settlement of Israel by the descendents of the Hebrews in Egypt, warfare, disease and famine threatened their extinction. For the survival of the Jews as a people, it became imperative for women to have many children while still participating as equals in the raising of crops. The rules of society which were formulated then, and which we recognize from the Bible, reflected the urgent reality of the need to be fruitful and multiply.

Women were in short supply because giving birth to many children increased risk of illness and death. We lived only about three-fourths as long as men. This increased our social value, but at the same time we did not live to the age of venerability to take on positions of community leadership and influence.

Eventually, changing social conditions no longer required the emphasis on domestic labor and high fertility for survival, but by then social customs and laws created by the male elders had become so ingrained that our limited role could not expand to suit the times. The development of cities broadened the business role of men, while women's economic contribution in peasant agriculture became less and less important. Thus our important role in perpetuating society through our

30

reproductive capacity became the excuse, rather than the cause for our lack of power.

Like the slaves in Egypt, we had assured the foundation of a strong society, but we had no hand in its direction.

We were slaves. In countless ways, we still dwell in Egypt.

Liberation Times Three
(A Supplemental Story)

Rifkah was born on her mother's kitchen floor while all of Krakow outside the shtetl were celebrating the beginning of the 20th century. Her father, the beloved rabbi, learned of the birth of his eighth daughter when he arrived home. He kissed his wife, glanced at the baby, and rushed back to his cherished scrolls.

By the time Rifkah was ten, she had barely seen her father at home. Her mother had given birth to six more girls, two of whom had been stillborn. Three days after Rifkah's birthday, her mother was delivered of a pale boy who died four days later in his father's arms. Her mother lingered for three months before she too, died. By then, all of the older daughters had married and moved out, leaving Rifkah to raise the remaining children. Four years later, at 14, Rifkah married. For her dowry, Father sent her mother's pots and her four younger sisters.

As she left her father's house, her cousin Sarah whispered: "May God go with you...you deserve to be liberated from this horrible life."

The next year Rifkah gave birth to fraternal twins. the boy survived. Within seven years, she was delivered of two daughters, two stillborn boys, and a son. Two days before her 24th birthday, she died.

Rifkah's husband of ten years refused to remarry. His eldest daughter, Hannah, aged nine, took over her mother's kitchen. Fifteen years later, as Hannah was lighting the Shabbos candles in front of her father, sister, brothers and their families, the door was kicked in by armed, shouting soldiers. Dragged out by her hair, she never saw her family again.

In 1945, other armed soldiers carried her gently outside the barbed wire, shouting, "You have been liberated!"

Hannah met Aaron in a D.P. camp and came to New York two years later as his wife. Aaron joined his uncle's garment factory; Hannah worked as the bookkeeper. They had four daughters. For each birth Aaron came home early, shortly joined by the rest of his joyful family, to celebrate the mitzvah.

When Hannah's grandchildren were past eight years old, immersed in piano, riding and ballet lessons, she realized that their mothers, her daughters, had returned to work. She complained: "You're allowing strangers to raise your children."

Her daughters patiently explained, "We need to work...to feel liberated..."

Hannah did not understand. She died six years later, two days after her seventieth birthday celebration, still not understanding what her daughters needed to be liberated from.

The Liberation from Egypt

"For the sake of righteous women, we were delivered from Egypt" [Rashi, Pesachim 108b].

The story of the liberation from Egypt begins with the heroism of two midwives — Shifrah and Puah. According to Torah, they refused to obey Pharaoh's command to kill male babies of Hebrew women whose birthings they attended. When Pharaoh called for them and questioned their contempt, they responded that the Hebrew women "are not as the Egyptian women; for they are lively, and are delivered ere the midwife come unto them" [Exodus 1:19].

One of the legends of our people* describes Miriam's central role in the exodus, and why she is called a prophetess. Miriam's name means "bitterness", and she was so called because of the bitterness of the Hebrews' lives in slavery.

Miriam's father, Amram, was head of the Hebrew council. When Pharaoh decreed his intention to kill all the male offspring of the Hebrews, Amram chose to cast his wife, Yocheved, aside, and many of his followers also divorced their wives.

*Angelo Rappoport, *Myth and Legend of Ancient Israel,* Vol. 2, KTAV Publishing House, Inc., 1966, Chapter XVII.

After several years, Miriam prophesied, "Another son shall be born to my parents; he shall free Israel from bondage and deliver them out of the hands of the Egyptians." She reproved her father, telling him that his decision to live apart from his wife was even more cruel than Pharaoh's decree.

"Pharaoh has in mind the destruction of the male children, while your decision would deprive the Hebrew nation of all posterity — female and male. It is unlikely that Pharaoh's decree will succeed, because he is wicked and unjust, but yours is likely to be upheld because you are so pious and good." This made sense to Amram, and he once more led Yocheved under the wedding canopy, while Miriam and her brother Aaron danced around it. Soon, the followers of Amram had remarried.

Shortly thereafter, Yocheved gave birth to a son. Great happiness filled the household, and it was felt Miriam's prophecy had materialized. The child was quiet, and was successfully hidden for three months in the Nile. "And his sister stood afar off, to know what would be done to him" [Exodus 2:4].

As Miriam watched, Pharaoh's daughter, Thermutis, plucked the baby from his hiding place. Miriam joined her entourage, and advised Thermutis of a Hebrew woman whom she could hire as a wet nurse. Thus did Miriam assure her brother's safe upbringing in the arms of his real mother, in the palace of Pharaoh.

L'MIR'YAM HA N'VIAH

Words by Randee Friedman
and Rabbi Lenore Bohm

Music to the tune
of Eliyahu Hanavi

L'Mi-r'-yam Ha- N'-vi-ah, L'Mi-r'-yam Ha

N'-vi-ah, Ul'-a-cho-tei-nu Sa-ra v' Riv-ka

A - nu not - not b' ra - a - cha

Alternative verses:
Ra-chel v'Lei-a...
Es-ter v'Di-na...
Shif-ra v'Pu-a...
Rut u'Dvo-ra...

To Miriam the Prophetess

To Miriam the Prophetess
And to our sisters:
Sarah and Rebekah,
Rachel and Leah,
Esther and Dinah,
Shifrah and Puah,
Ruth and Deborah,
We offer a blessing.

One day, when Moses was a grown man, he came upon an Egyptian beating a Hebrew. Moses fatally struck the Egyptian, then fled from Egypt and dwelt in the land of Midian.

Later, as he was guarding sheep, the voice of God spoke to Moses from a burning bush, saying, "I will send thee unto Pharaoh, that thou mayest bring forth My people the Children of Israel out of Egypt" [Exodus 3:10].

Again and again Moses stood before Pharaoh, demanding, "Let my people go!" But Pharaoh's heart was hardened.

We cried unto the Lord and the Lord heard our voice and saw our affliction and our toil and our oppression.

ALL:
And the Lord brought us out of Egypt with a mighty hand and with an outstretched arm and with great terror and with signs and wonders.

Plague after plague was sent upon the Egyptians. In compassion and sorrow over the evil and suffering that exists in the world, our ancestors in numbering the plagues, poured away with each one a drop of their wine of rejoicing.

There were ten plagues which the Lord brought upon the Egyptians: blood, frogs, vermin, flies, cattle disease, boils, hail, locusts, darkness, and killing of the first born.

These plagues played a necessary part in the liberation of Jews from slavery. Today, we Jewish women have still not completely gained our freedom.

EACH WOMAN POURS A DROP OF WINE ONTO
HER PLATE AS THE PLAGUES OF JEWISH
WOMEN ARE DESCRIBED.

Read together

These are the ten plagues brought upon women in
Jewish life:

1) The consistently male image of God.
2) The lack of recognition of women rabbis, cantors,
   scholars, and decision makers who could serve as
   models for all of us.
3) The biblical stories traditionally selected for commentary which neglect the role of women.
4) The sexist language of most prayers and blessings.
5) The repressive divorce laws, and the exclusion of
   women as witnesses in a Jewish court.
6) The education of our young women not being taken
   as seriously as that of our young men.
7) The lack of equality in salary and promotional
   opportunities for women in Jewish education and
   community service.

8) The devaluation of Jewish womanhood after the childbearing years are over.
9) The denial by omission of single women, childless women, battered women, lesbians, the elderly, the poor and the disabled from among the central concerns of organized Judaism.
10) The prison created by the rigid traditional views of men and women.

From these plagues, Judaism and women must be freed.

LIFT THE SECOND CUP OF WINE
(BUT DO NOT DRINK), AND SAY:

From these plagues upon our lives, we seek redemption.

DAYEINU

Had God only taken us out from the bondage of Egypt it would have been enough.

Alternative verses:
1) Ilu natan lanu et hashabat, dayeinu.
2) Ilu natan lanu et hatorah, dayeinu.

In traditional haggadot, we express our gratitude for all that was done for our people from the time we fled Egypt until the Temple was built in Israel. Each of these blessings alone "would have been sufficient" (dayeinu). However, it is a sign of powerlessness typical of oppressed people to resign ourselves after each fateful experience by saying "it could have been worse." It is important for us not only to be grateful for all the good things that have happened, but also to not settle for less than our full due as human beings.

Dayeinu?
(Would it have been enough?)

Had women been remembered equally with men
But forgotten in the telling of the exodus, dayeinu?
Had women been remembered in the telling of
the exodus
But not thought of as individuals, dayeinu?
Had women been thought of as individuals
But not seated among the men in synagogue, dayeinu?
Had women been seated among the men in synagogue
But not counted for a minyan, dayeinu?
Had women had been counted for a minyan
But not permitted an aliyah, dayeinu?
Had women been permitted an aliyah
But not been allowed to study Torah, dayeinu?
Had women been allowed to study Torah
But not become Bat Mitzvah, dayeinu?
Had women become Bat Mitzvah
But not gained access to the rabbinate, dayeinu?
Had women gained access to the rabbinate
But not been treated as complete equals, dayeinu?

When we are treated as complete equals,
then will men and women
go out from Egypt together!
Dayeinu, Dayeinu!

When even the Pharaoh's own first-born son was stricken in the final plague, Pharaoh arose in the night, called for Moses, and commanded him, "Get you forth from among my people!" [Exodus 12:31] In great haste the Children of Israel departed. When they came to the Red Sea, Pharaoh again broke his word, for his chariots pursued them.

The Lord caused the waters to be divided and the Israelites passed over safely; then the waters closed on the Egyptians with their chariots of war. Thus the Children of Israel became free.

Let us remember and never forget: The promise of God to deliver our people has been kept again and again, throughout the ages. For forces have risen against us to destroy us not only this once, but in every generation.

Seeing that they had been saved, the Hebrew people rejoiced.

HODU

Psalm 118:1-4   Music by Debbie Friedman

Ho - du L'A-do-nai ki

tov, ki l' o - lam chas'do

ki l' o - lam chas' - do.   Fine

Yo-mar na, yo-mar na Yis'- ra ---

eil ki l' o - lam chas'do

ki l' o - lam chas do. Yom'ru na

yom'ru na 1. vait A - ha - ron ki l'
                2. Yir'ei A - do - nai

o - lam chas'do, ki l' o lam chas'do.

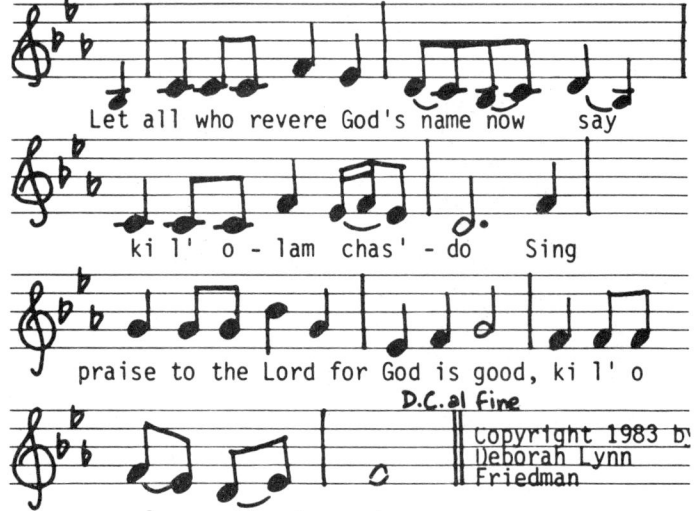

Let all who revere God's name now say

ki l' o - lam chas' - do   Sing

praise to the Lord for God is good, ki l' o

D.C. al Fine

Copyright 1983 by
Deborah Lynn
Friedman

lam   chas' - do.

"And Miriam the prophetess, the sister of Aaron, took a timbrel in her hand; and all the women went out after her with timbrels and with dances. And Miriam sang unto them" [Exodus 15:20, 21].

SHIRU LA-ADONAI

Exodus 15:21
Lyrics modified from ... Rabbi Lynn Gottlieb

Music by

Shi-ru la-A-do-nai ki ga-oh ga-ah,

sus v'roch'-vo ra - ma va - yam.

Sing to A-do-nai whose glo-ry thun-ders,

all the might-y war-riors cast in the

sea which gave us birth.

There is a story in our tradition about the Egyptians who drowned:

When the Israelites crossed over safely, the Angels in Heaven began to sing in praise of God. But God looked down upon the waters closing over the Egyptians, and cried, "How can you sing when my children are drowning?" [Megillah 10b]

From the Red Sea, Moses led Israel inland. They crossed the desert and dwelt for a time in an oasis in tents. Early in their wandering they came into the wilderness of Sinai and camped. Moses went up on the Mount, where he received God's commandments:

"I am the Lord thy God, who brought thee out of the land of Egypt, out of the house of bondage.

Thou shalt have no other gods
    before Me...
Thou shalt not take the name of
    the Lord thy God in vain...
Remember the sabbath day, to
    keep it holy...
Honor thy father and thy mother...
Thou shalt not murder.
Thou shalt not commit adultery.
Thou shalt not steal.
Thou shalt not bear false witness
    against thy neighbor.
Thou shalt not covet..."
[Exodus 20:2-14]

This is the word of God as embodied
on our Torah.

Rachatsa
(washing of hands by everyone)

רָחְצָה

בָּרוּךְ אַתָּה יְיָ אֱלֹהֵינוּ מֶלֶךְ
הָעוֹלָם אֲשֶׁר קִדְּשָׁנוּ בְּמִצְוֹתָיו וְצִוָּנוּ
עַל־נְטִילַת יָדָיִם:

Baruch Ata, Adonai Eloheinu, melech ha-olam,
asher kid'shanu b'mitsvotav v'tsivanu al-n'tilat
yadayim.

Blessed are You, our God, Creator of the Universe,
Who makes us holy with mitsvot and commands
us concerning the washing of the hands.

   The second cup of wine is to the Law, which acts as
a basis for our ethical conduct toward one another.

Lift the wine cup, saying: *2nd of blessing*

בָּרוּךְ אַתָּה יְיָ, אֱלֹהֵינוּ מֶלֶךְ הָעוֹלָם,
בּוֹרֵא פְּרִי הַגָּפֶן.

Baruch Ata, Adonai Eloheinu, melech ha-olam,
borei p'ri hagafen.

Blessed are You, our God, Sovereign of the Universe,
Creator of the fruit of the vine.

ALL DRINK THE SECOND CUP OF WINE.

54

Motsi Matsa
(blessing and eating the matsa)

מוֹצִיא
מַצָּה

We are now coming to the Seder meal. As we ordinarily begin with the breaking of bread, we begin tonight with the breaking of matsa.

HOLD UP THE FOURTH MATSA

This is the Matsa of Hope.
This matsa symbolizes the indestructible links between us and all Jews who are victims of tyranny and oppression. For those who are not able to observe this holy time, their struggle shall be heard! We will add our voice to theirs, and together our voices will be joined by all people of conscience.
Until all Jews are free, no Jew is free.

ALL BREAK OFF A SMALL PORTION OF CEREMONIAL MATSA, SAYING:

בָּרוּךְ אַתָּה יְיָ אֱלֹהֵינוּ מֶלֶךְ הָעוֹלָם הַמּוֹצִיא
לֶחֶם מִן הָאָרֶץ:

Baruch Ata, Adonai Eloheinu, melech ha-olam,
hamotsi lechem min ha-arets.

Blessed are You, our God, Creator of the Universe, who brings forth bread from the earth.

בָּרוּךְ אַתָּה יְיָ, אֱלֹהֵינוּ מֶלֶךְ הָעוֹלָם,
אֲשֶׁר קִדְּשָׁנוּ בְּמִצְוֹתָיו, וְצִוָּנוּ עַל
אֲכִילַת מַצָּה.

Baruch Ata, Adonai Eloheinu, melech ha-olam,
asher kid'shanu b'mitsvotav v'tsivanu al achilat
matsa.

Blessed are You, our God, Creator of the Universe,
who makes us holy with mitsvot and commands us
to eat unleavened bread.

EVERYONE EAT THE MATSA.

Maror
(blessing and eating the bitter herb)

מָרוֹר

Now we each will take a bit of the bitter herb to
fulfill the commandment of this night to eat the bitter
herb.

בָּרוּךְ אַתָּה יְיָ, אֱלֹהֵינוּ מֶלֶךְ הָעוֹלָם,
אֲשֶׁר קִדְּשָׁנוּ בְּמִצְוֹתָיו, וְצִוָּנוּ עַל
אֲכִילַת מָרוֹר.

Baruch Ata, Adonai Eloheinu, melech ha-olam,
asher kid'shanu b'mitsvotav v'tsivanu al achilat
maror.

Blessed are You, our God, Creator of the Universe,
who makes us holy with mits'vot and commands us to
eat bitter herbs.

EVERYONE EATS THE MAROR ON MATSA.

It says in the Mishnah, the collection of Jewish law included in the Talmud, in the section Pesachim, that it is incumbent upon each person gathered at a Seder to recite the following words:

בְּכָל דּוֹר וָדוֹר חַיָּב אָדָם לִרְאוֹת אֶת עַצְמוֹ כְּאִילּוּ הוּא יָצָא מִמִּצְרָיִם.

"B'chol dor vador chayav adam lir'ot et'ats'mo k'ilu hu yatsa mimits'rayim."

"In all generations it is the duty of man to consider himself as if he had come forth from Egypt."

This sentence is a stumbling block for any woman reciting at a Seder who wishes to fully understand what it means to be "free" as a Jew. For a woman, Jewish freedom means to be able to respond completely as a mature practicing adult to any issues which arise within the Jewish community.

How can a woman recite "ats'mo" (himself) and still feel she is an adult decision maker? If she can, she does not yet fully understand what it means to go out from slavery to freedom. She is still second class — a woman walking in a man's footsteps, a child who needs to be recited for, a girl fearing and trembling, unable to express herself in the language of an adult female Jew.

Freedom can only be gained by a woman when she herself becomes fully knowledgeable and fully capable of speaking and acting for herself. And this means, whenever necessary, actively, not passively, extracting herself from Pharaoh's grip — in whatever guise or form that hold takes place. And if in the process of discovery she finds that she is in part pharaoh to herself, she must renew the struggle yearly until such time comes when she can stand at a Seder and recite for herself:

בְּכָל דּוֹר וָדוֹר חַיֶּבֶת אִשָּׁה לִרְאוֹת אֶת עַצְמָה כְּאִלּוּ
הִיא יָצְאָה מִמִּצְרַיִם.

"B'chol dor vador chayevet isha lir'ot et'ats'ma
k'ilu hi yatsa mimits'rayim."

In all generations it is the duty of a woman to consider herself as if she had come forth from Egypt.

58

Koreich
(combining matsa and maror)

Tradition adds one more custom, in honor of the great teacher Hillel, head of the rabbinic academy in Jerusalem at the time of the Romans. A non-Jew asked the rabbi to teach him the entire Torah while he stood on one foot. Hillel said, "Do unto others what you would have them do unto you. That is the whole Torah. The rest is commentary. Now go and study."

On Passover, Hillel followed precisely the instruction about the sanctified lamb. "Upon unleavened bread and bitter herbs shall they eat it." So he placed a bit of the pascal offering on the matsa, with bitter herbs. In remembrance of the Temple and Hillel, we shall place the bitter herb with charoset on the matsa.

EVERYONE EATS HER "HILLEL SANDWICH".

The teaching is completed with one exception, and then we may come to the meal. It was a grandchild of Rabbi Hillel, Rabbi Gamaliel, who gave us the rule for when we may eat the feast. "He or she who has not talked about these three things," he said more or less, "has not fulfilled the obligation to observe the Passover. They are the shank bone, the matsa and the maror." We have explained all three, so let us begin the Passover feast with these words:

A WOMAN'S SEDER

It starts a week before.
Each drawer, each shelf,
   is stripped and scrubbed;
A rite performed each spring
   since Pharaoh forced
The chosen ones to flee
   before their bread could rise.
I wash a dish, streaked black
   from last year's news
And filled with years of
   family seders,
And think of Miriam,
The woman who began
Our journey to the promised land.

Did she lament the flat and
    tasteless bread
She served her men?
Or did she know that we
    would share her deed
Each spring as we recall
    her exodus from bondage,
That has still to be complete?
As smells of spring
    and chicken soup mix pleasingly,
I peel an apple, chop the nuts,
    and sip the wine,
Remembering the bricks
    that stood between
Each ghetto girl and study
of the Torah.
The shankbone roasts
    and fills the air
Within my modern home
With smells of sacrifice
    that women made
So that there would be Seders
    every year.
I fill a dish with bitter herbs,
But feel no bitterness,
Because I know that
    each small task links me
With every Hebrew woman
    who prepared
A Seder meal since God proclaimed
    that Jews
Should celebrate their freedom
    every year.

Surely God never meant
For women to be passed over.

WOMANSIDE

© 1982

Music and lyrics
by Robyn Samuels

Bring out the wo-man-side, hon-or the wo-man-side, we all have a wo - man - side wo - men and men. Bring out the wo-man - side, nur-ture the wo-man - side, Someday the world will be bal-anced a-gain.

Shul-chan Oreich
(the festive meal)

DURING THE MEAL, HIDE THE AFIKOMAN.
AT THE MEAL'S END, THE THIRD CUP
OF WINE IS FILLED.

Tsafun
(finding the Afikoman)

צָפוּן

Now you may hunt for the afikoman.

MIRIAM'S CUP IS MYSTERIOUSLY DRAINED
DURING THE SEARCH.

THE AFIKOMAN IS MATCHED WITH THE
OTHER PART OF THE MATSA FROM THE
PLATE.

What is broken shall be made whole. What is shattered
shall be restored. Our hope is ourselves, to find what is
lost, to bring together what is broken, to restore
our faith.

DISTRIBUTE AND EAT THE AFIKOMAN.

Birkat Hamazon
(blessing after the meal)

בִּרְכַּת הַמָּזוֹן

LEADER:

רַבּוֹתַי נְבָרֵךְ

Rabotai n'vareich.

Let us say grace.

ALL:

יְהִי שֵׁם יְיָ מְבֹרָךְ מֵעַתָּה וְעַד־עוֹלָם:

Y'hi sheim Adonai m'vorach mei-ata v'ad olam.

May the name of God be blessed from now throughout eternity.

(LEADER REPEATS)

LEADER:

בִּרְשׁוּת מָרָנָן וְרַבָּנָן וְרַבּוֹתַי נְבָרֵךְ
אֱלֹהֵינוּ שֶׁאָכַלְנוּ מִשֶּׁלּוֹ:

Bir'shut maranan v'rabanan v'rabotai n'vareich
Eloheinu she-achal'nu mishelo.

Let us praise God, Who has provided us with such bounty.

ALL:

בָּרוּךְ אֱלֹהֵינוּ שֶׁאָכַלְנוּ מִשֶּׁלּוֹ וּבְטוּבוֹ חָיִינוּ:

Baruch Eloheinu she-achal'nu mishelo uv'tuvo chayinu.

Let us praise God, in Whose goodness we live.

(LEADER REPEATS)

ALL:

בָּרוּךְ הוּא וּבָרוּךְ שְׁמוֹ:

בָּרוּךְ אַתָּה יְיָ אֱלֹהֵינוּ מֶלֶךְ הָעוֹלָם, הַזָּן אֶת הָעוֹלָם כֻּלּוֹ
בְּטוּבוֹ, בְּחֵן בְּחֶסֶד וּבְרַחֲמִים. הוּא נוֹתֵן לֶחֶם לְכָל בָּשָׂר, כִּי
לְעוֹלָם חַסְדּוֹ. וּבְטוּבוֹ הַגָּדוֹל תָּמִיד לֹא חָסַר לָנוּ, וְאַל יֶחְסַר
לָנוּ מָזוֹן לְעוֹלָם וָעֶד בַּעֲבוּר שְׁמוֹ הַגָּדוֹל. כִּי הוּא אֵל זָן
וּמְפַרְנֵס לַכֹּל, וּמֵטִיב לַכֹּל, וּמֵכִין מָזוֹן לְכָל בְּרִיּוֹתָיו אֲשֶׁר
בָּרָא. בָּרוּךְ אַתָּה, יְיָ, הַזָּן אֶת הַכֹּל.

Baruch hu uvaruch sh'mo. Baruch Ata, Adonai
Eloheinu, melech ha-olam, hazan et ha-olam kulo
b'tuvo b'chein b'chesed uv'rachamim hu notein lechem
l'chol basar ki l'olam chas'do. Uv'tuvo hagadol tamid
lo chasar lanu v'al yech'sar lanu mazon l'olam va-ed
ba-avur sh'mo hagadol. Ki hu eil zan um'far'neis lakol
umeitiv lakol umeichin mazon l'chol b'riyotav asher
bara. Baruch Ata Adonai, hazan et hakol.

Blessed are You, our God, Provider for the Universe,
Who sustains the whole world with loving kindness and
mercy. You give food to all creatures. With goodness
and grace you have fed us. Thank you God, for
continuing to nourish all your people.

ALL:

וּבְנֵה יְרוּשָׁלַיִם עִיר הַקֹּדֶשׁ בִּמְהֵרָה בְיָמֵינוּ.
בָּרוּךְ אַתָּה, יְיָ, בּוֹנֵה בְרַחֲמָיו יְרוּשָׁלָיִם, אָמֵן.

Uv'nei Y'rushalayim ir hakodesh bim'heira v'yameinu.
Baruch Ata Adonai, boneh v'rachamav Y'rushalayim.
Amein.

Build Jerusalem, our God, speedily in our day. We
praise God, Whose compassion builds Jerusalem.

ALL:

עֹשֶׂה שָׁלוֹם בִּמְרוֹמָיו הוּא יַעֲשֶׂה שָׁלוֹם
עָלֵינוּ וְעַל כָּל־יִשְׂרָאֵל. וְאִמְרוּ אָמֵן:
יְיָ עֹז לְעַמּוֹ יִתֵּן, יְיָ יְבָרֵךְ אֶת־עַמּוֹ
בַשָּׁלוֹם:

Oseh shalom bim'romav hu ya'ase shalom aleinu
v'al kol Yis'raeil. V'im'ru, amein. Adonai oz l'amo
yitein, Adonai y'vareich et amo vashalom.

May God Who brings harmony to all the universe
bring peace on earth for all humankind. God will
give strength to all people. God will bless all humankind
with peace.

LIFT THE THIRD CUP OF WINE AND SAY:

בָּרוּךְ אַתָּה יְיָ אֱלֹהֵינוּ מֶלֶךְ הָעוֹלָם בּוֹרֵא פְּרִי הַגָּפֶן:

Baruch Ata, Adonai Eloheinu, melech ha-olam,
borei p'ri hagafen.

Blessed are You, our God,
Sovereign of the Universe,
Creator of the fruit of the vine.

DRINK THE THIRD CUP OF WINE

It is the Celebration
of God's Passover

After a time, your children will say to you,
 "What do you mean by this service?"
And you will say,
 "It is the blessing of God's Passover."

We do this because God showed our foremothers
 a mighty strength, and gave us a heritage
 which we celebrate.
And you will say,
 "It is the meaning of God's Passover."

We see God's strong hand
 made manifest in Sarah's laughter,
 in the pain of Rebekah's two nations,
 and in the desire of Rachel's heart.
And you will say,
 "It is the lesson of God's Passover."

We feel the fear in Leah's eyes,
 we bear with Dinah's rape, we rise in Shifrah's arms,
 and stand firm in Puah's lies.
And you will say,
 "It is the offering of God's Passover."

We grow with the labors of Yocheved,
 and are taught by the voice of Miriam,
 and pray with Zipporah
 as she cut the foreskin of her son.
And you will say,
 "It is the history of God's Passover."

We see once again the first born
smitten in the hand of Jael,
the guile of Judith, and the temper of Esther.
And you will say,
"It is the nature of God's Passover."

As it was with the women of the first Passover,
so it was with Hannah Senesh and her flame,
and with Zivia Lubetkin in the Warsaw ghetto,
and with the unnamed mothers of the death camps.
And you will say,
"It is the sacrifice of God's Passover."

And so we remember what will challenge
the Rule of the Unrighteous on Pesach:
"Thy hand shall be mighty, thy right arm uplifted,
as on the night of the hallowing of the Passover."
And you will say,
"It is the power of God's Passover."

OPEN THE DOOR FOR MIRIAM
THE PROPHETESS

We are told that Miriam the prophetess visits every house where a woman's seder is being held. We open the door to welcome her. Eagerly we await her arrival. As we think of Miriam, we admire her unusual strength and courage, and give honor to a great leader.

As we open the door on this Seder evening, we are also mindful of its being a symbol of hospitality and friendliness; as a sign that no woman is shut off from other human beings; and as a symbol for all women who are going forth with dignity and pride into the making of a Jewish future for all our people.

CLOSE THE DOOR

Hallel
(Psalms of praise)

הַלֵּל

HAL'LUYA

Psalm 113

Ha - l'- lu - ya, ha-l'lu - ya, ha-l'-
lu av'- dei A-do - nai. Ha-l' - lu-ya,
ha-l'-lu - ya, ha-l'- lu et sheim A-do- nai.
Ha-l'-lu - ya, ha-l'-lu - ya, ha-l'-
lu-ya, ha - l'-lu - ya. Let all that
live sing praises to God. Ha-l' - lu - ya.

הַלְלוּיָהּ, הַלְלוּיָהּ, הַלְלוּ עַבְדֵי אֲדֹנָי,
הַלְלוּיָהּ, הַלְלוּיָהּ, הַלְלוּ אֶת שֵׁם אֲדֹנָי.

הַלְלוּיָהּ.

Nir'tsa
(accepting God's covenant)

FILL AND LIFT THE FOURTH CUP OF WINE.

As we drink the last cup of wine, we recall our covenant with God, and accept the responsibility and the privilege of being a Jew.

בָּרוּךְ אַתָּה יְיָ אֱלֹהֵינוּ מֶלֶךְ הָעוֹלָם בּוֹרֵא פְּרִי הַגָּפֶן:

Baruch Ata, Adonai Eloheinu, melech ha-olam,
borei p'ri hagafen.

Blessed are You, our God, Sovereign of the Universe,
Creator of the fruit of the vine.

Our commemoration of Passover is now accomplished. May we celebrate Passover next year in a world at peace. May courageous steps be taken to bring peace and cooperation between Israel and her neighbors. May we all make continuous strides towards friendship and sisterhood. May we celebrate Passover next year in a world of universal freedom for women and for men.

לְשָׁנָה הַבָּאָה בִּירוּשָׁלָיִם:

L'shana haba-a biy'rushalayim!

Next year in Jerusalem!

IM TIR'TSU

Lyrics by Theodore Herzl and
Naphtali Herz Imber (from Hatikvah)

Music by Debbie
Friedman © 1983

Im tir'-tsu, im tir'tsu

ein zo a-ga-da,

ein zo a-ga-da Li-h'-yot

am chof'-shi b' - ar - tsei - nu

b' - e - rets tsi - yon

bi - ru-sha-la - yim

If you will it, it is no legend;
to be a free people in our land,
in Zion and Jerusalem.

LO YISA GOI

Isaiah 2:4

Folk Tune

Lo yi-sa goi el goi che-rev
lo yil'·m'-du od mil'·cha - ma.
Lo yi-sa goi el goi che - rev
lo yil'm'-du od mil' cha-ma.

Nation shall not lift up sword
against nation, nor ever again
shall they train for war.

HINEI MA TOV

Adapted from Psalm 133:1   Traditional tune

Hi-nei ma tov u - ma na - im

she'vet a-chot gam ya-chad, hi-nei ma tov u-

Fine

ma na - im she-vet a-chot gam ya-chad.

Hi-nei ma tov, hi-nei ma tov, La la

la la la la la la la la. Hi-

nei ma tov u - ma na - im she-vet a-chot

gam ya-chad, hi - nei ma tov u - ma na-im

she-vet a-chot gam ya-chad. Hi- nei ma tov

Behold how good and how pleasant
it is for sisters to dwell together.

FOR WOMEN EVERYWHERE

Words and music by the Zimbabwe YWCA   1985
for the International Women's Conference, Nairobi

All a-cross the nations, all a-round the world

wo-men are long-ing to be free. No

long-er in the sha-dows, forced to stay behind, but

side by side in true e-qual-i - ty. So

sing a song for wo - men ev'-ry-

where; let it ring a-round the world & never, never

cease. Sing a song for wo-men ev'ry-

where: e - qual-i-ty, de-vel-op - ment and peace.

(2) Women can't be silent when all around the world
people hurt and hungry children cry.
We'll sing out now for justice, and development
And hold the rights of all the people high.

Chorus: (So sing a song, for women everywhere...)

(3) Women now are working to build a better world,
where the dove of peace can rest on every shore,
where men lay down their weapons and learn to
love and share,
and people work to bring an end to war.

Chorus

Notes to the Leader of the Seder

Ask any Jewish adult to conjure up memories of Jewish experiences from childhood, and chances are good that a Passover Seder will be part of those memories. The Seder is one of the most universally celebrated Jewish rituals, even for those who do not observe other traditions.

Memories of the Seder table laden with ritual objects, the aroma of delicious foods, the sounds of the Seder — songs, voices of relatives — these are all powerful images even after many years. Add to this the image of a father or grandfather at the head of the table, leading the Seder with a firm but loving hand, and you have a picture that many can recall.

As the leader of a women's Seder you must begin your preparations by imagining a picture that is very different from the one just described in two important respects. First, this is not a Seder of family members but rather the gathering of an extended family, the family of women. Some of the participants may know each other but others may not. Second, this is one Seder that is not presided over by father or grandfather. For many, this will be their first experience at a Seder led by women. Therefore the dynamics of the group will be different from a family gathering.

It is important to accept these differences as the realities of the celebration and not be inhibited by them. Above all, you should not feel obligated to conduct a Seder that is a carbon copy of Seders you have attended in the past. Use previous experiences, but inject your own spirit and talents into this women's Seder. Make it memorable, for that is one of the reasons for holding a women's Seder. We celebrate our liberation from Egypt and acknowledge our role as women in people's history.

In preparing to conduct the Seder, first read through the Haggadah thoroughly. Familiarize yourself with the sequence of the Seder (which parallels other Haggadot), the readings and the rituals connected with the Seder in general and this Haggadah in particular. As the leader, determine how the Seder will be conducted. We suggest that you use a variety of techniques to encourage and maximize participation by all in attendance. Some passages can be read by individuals, while others can be recited in unison or responsively.

You have the option of using Hebrew, English or a combination of both. You can also decide what, if any, additional readings you want to integrate. While the Haggadah is your map for the Seder, you have the freedom to add what is appropriate and use what is meaningful for your group.

If you are fortunate enough to have a songleader, be sure to go over all the music with her before the Seder. Determine what songs to include, which melodies to use, and when, during the Seder, the singing will take place.

Seating arrangement is an important consideration. While lack of space may limit the alternatives, keep in mind that the placement of the table can either enhance or inhibit participation of the group. It is preferable, we have found, to have one long connected table rather than a series of separate tables. This adds to the cohesiveness of the group as the Seder service proceeds.

In addition to the many themes that are part of the Seder, choosing a unique focus can be enriching. As was mentioned in the introduction, one year the Institute emphasized intergenerational participation. The leader had her eight-year-old daughter help conduct the service. Many women brought their mothers or mothers-in-law with them. Also, as each woman introduced herself, she mentioned foremothers or children who joined us in spirit for our women's Seder.

Just as family Seders develop their own traditions, so, too, can a women's Seder. One of the special traditions of the Institute's Seders is to embroider the name of the Seder leader and songleader on the pillow against which the leader reclines. In addition, the leader might encourage the women to share personal liberation stories over dinner or to relate especially fond memories of previous Passovers.

Depending upon the organization of your Seder, it may also be the responsibility of the leader to gather the necessary ritual items, which will include:

- SEDER PLATE OR PLATES
  karpas (greens)
  shank bone
  maror (bitter herbs)
  charoset (apples,nuts, wine)
  egg (first hardboiled, then roasted
      in its shell)
- MATSA PLATE
  three ceremonial matsot and matsa of hope
  matsa cover
  matsot to accompany ceremony and meal
- HAGGADOT (for all participants)
- BOWLS OF SALT WATER
- WINE CUPS AND WINE
- BOWLS WITH WATER (for hand-washing ritual)
- CANDLES AND CANDLEHOLDERS
- CUP FOR MIRIAM THE PROPHETESS
- PILLOW FOR THE LEADER

Now you are ready to lead your women's Seder.

Your additional songs, prayers, ceremonies or stories.